A BOAT
for the
SINKING

P O E M S   B Y
BRANDON WHITE

Raw Earth Ink

2023

This book is a work of poetry.

First paperback edition March 2023

All photographs and digital art by Brandon White
Cover and interior design by tara caribou

ISBN 979-8-98660-528-9 (paperback)

Published by Raw Earth Ink
PO Box 39332
Ninilchik, AK 99639
www.raw-earth-ink.com

For Kenzie and our little birds

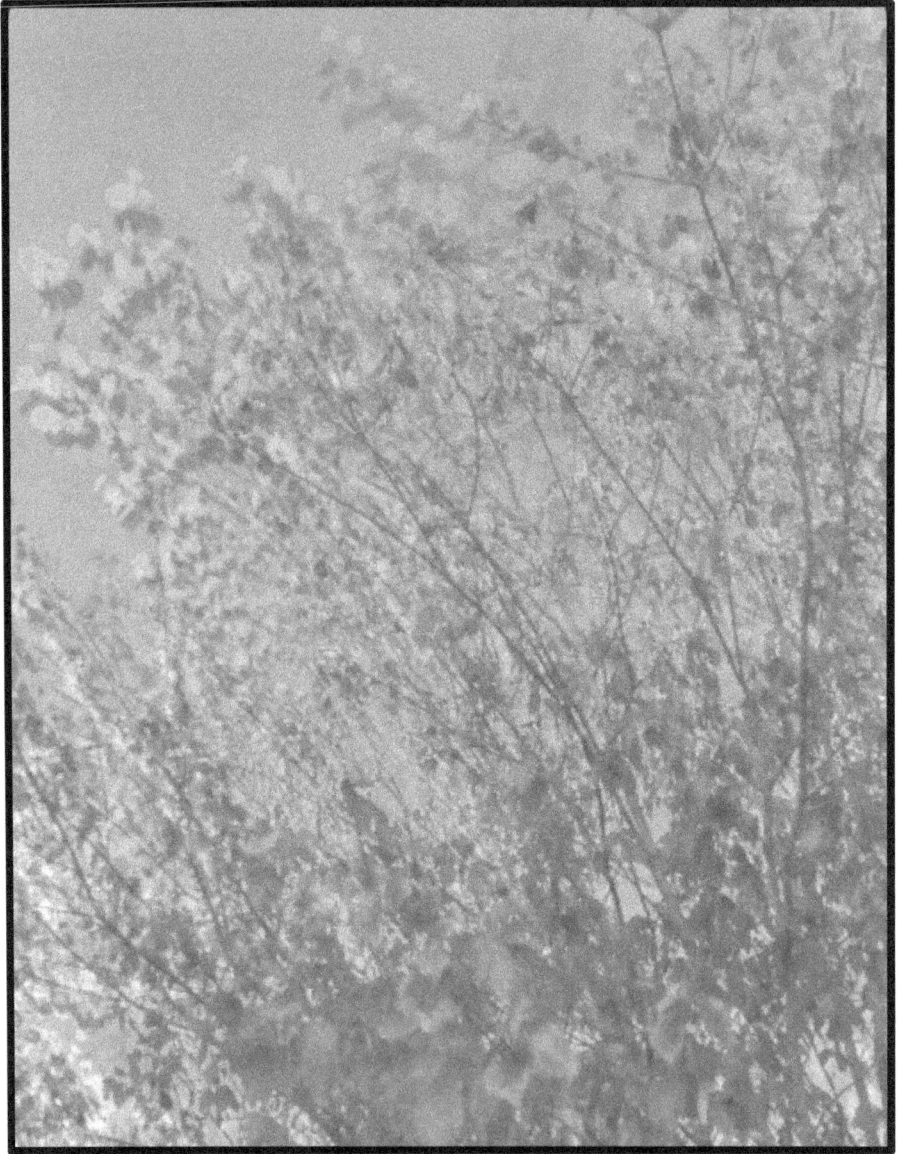

Take this heart

and set a course

for better days

Coffee, Poetry, Fetch

Is this what you'll remember

in what I hope is many years

from now?

On another back porch,

with another dog,

another stick,

another book,

another winter,

warmed by the laughter

of your child

and strong coffee?

When I'm the cardinal

perched on the branch,

and my face comes

in fiery flashes

of memory?

Will you think of the fence?

The cold of the concrete

seeping through your socks?

The low bark

of the wild-eyed Catahoula

begging for another throw?

I'll find you there

I'll fold my wings neatly

and sing a song

of what's to come

Their Eyes Beyond

I drive myself crazy
imagining ways
to pierce the veil

How the mind might
be used to fold and tear
the fabric of perception

that one might peek through
to the world beyond
the wool

Consider our limitations;
how few colors and frequencies
the mind can endure

Dare we open our arms
to what we can
only hope to comprehend?

To that which is,
has been,
and will be?

Before you, before I,
were known before
knowing?

Before the first pair of eyes
set skyward,
before a mind wondered;

What waits for us?
Or, perhaps more
importantly,

who?

Slush

My simple, frozen world
lays dreaming of
the sun

while tires search for asphalt
beneath the ice,
craving friction,

a little momentum,
a little heat,
something familiar

I'm slipping and sliding
and thinking of how you
left no trace

how you passed
through my life
like a dream

when I should
be focusing on
the road

No Explanation

Outside this window,
the cycle continues
without my participation,
without my permission,
without regard

Inside it's heartburn
and headache, the silence
only interrupted by my phone
dancing across the nightstand,
lit up with condolences

All this time and still
in love with my brokenness;
addicted to the shame
that comes when I consider
moving on

This morning, I tried
to explain heaven
and stopped
halfway
through

Self

Reflecting on
the nature of my heart,
this caged bird singing,
what is this lack of
gratitude?

The endless
internal war of self,
I'm all blood and guts
on the inside,

aren't you?

The Smell of Rain

Step into the day
and into the cool air
charged with rumors
of rain

this is what's missed,
the gathering storm
humming electric,
pure and threatening

What could stoke
the flame of wonder
like the hands of
God?

Do you kneel
to the natural forces?
That was a rhetorical
question

The dancing trees,
the blades of grass,
the wild horse in its running,
man and his wild confusion;

All eyes turn to
the darkening clouds

War on Mute

Scenes of intense battle
fill this living room,
these quiet hours

Heroes die
in slow motion,
never screaming

Exit wounds
bursting like
confetti poppers

painting the world
in the color
of love

Withdrawal

If I sweat through this shirt
that'll make two

The pills can't touch
the ache behind my eyes

and I'm wondering if you
can tell that I'm pretending

Outside, an infestation
of bikers eats my town alive

and I'm feeling
confused

I'm forgetting names
and dates

I've gathered every memory
of my Father

into one place and locked
the door behind me

I put a finger to my lips
and beg them

not to make
a sound

Gathering

This is
the gathering season

Creative
output is a slow drip

as the mind
gathers material together

that will later
be fashioned

into poems
about whatever

At the End of the Day

It might be a heart attack
in the liquor store parking lot
because it feels like more
than anxiety this time

I downloaded an app
to test my heart rate
and it tells me
I'm in the green

What does it say about me
that I would allow my phone
to determine the seriousness
of this or any situation?

My job requires me
to face the world,
so, I chew little white footballs
to avoid coming apart

I don't write about
what I do for money,
because it has nothing
to do with anything

other than my heart

<u>Muse</u>

In the grand scheme
you were
momentary

and now
I keep you
like a proper poet

at the borders
of the mind,
in flashes

of cold
memory

Exit 8

The sky
was an oil painting
and I was stoned
and terrified
doing 80
down I-40,
as close
to Hunter S. Thompson
as I'll ever be

In between
moments of panic,
I thought of poetry and art
and how old men confused
by such things
are just afraid
of being swallowed up
by a world that never cared
if it was understood

I squeal like a child
on Exit 8
I spun round and round,
careless and unworthy
of my blessings,
and wrapped in the arms
of my shame
when the car straightened
I wiped away tears

<u>Shards</u>

I haven't thought of the phone calls
since making them three years ago
Aunts and Uncle, sisters, my boss,

my shaky voice delivers the message:

He's gone. It's over.

It being suffering and false hope

We were left with shards of a life,
looking them over in bewilderment
until the words finally came:

Where do we even begin?

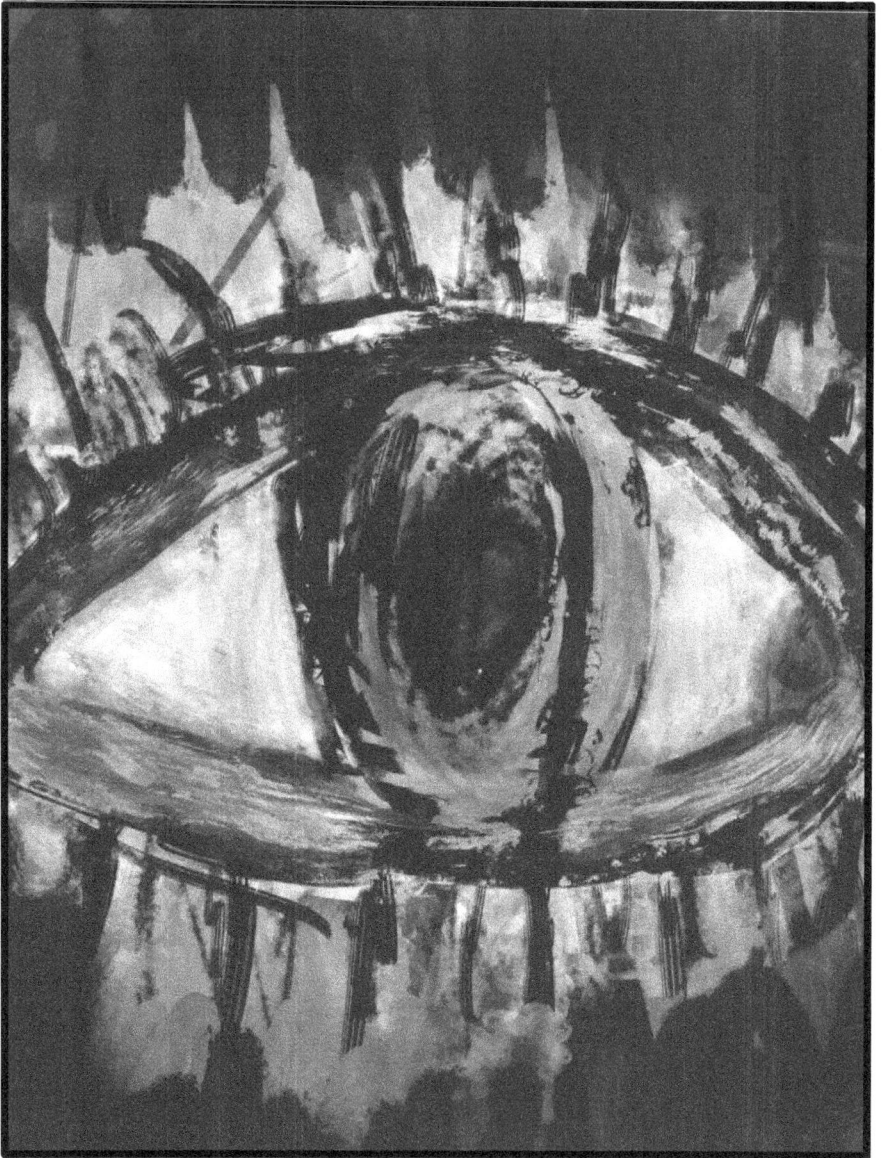

How to say it…

I've forgotten how

to live with myself.

Unfinished

Chain fried chicken
and fresh stress,
chasing dollars like I swore
I never would

That was pre-children
and prior to our family death explosion
that sent everything familiar
in a thousand different directions

Red light
Stop and stare
into unfamiliar eyes
reflecting
on old dreams

searching for a pulse

I need to get clean,
get clear

So many
unfinished things,
stirring
somewhere

Ease

I want
to melt
into how
I feel
right now

Everything
All at once
For me

Forever

Orbit

You're a satellite

miles away
but always in orbit   .

I imagine the grooves
of your palms

punched through
like Christ

I've been living
on stress

dreaming of
resets and endings

I imagine
you're blooming by now

wanting for
nothing

Impossible

mornings

Sun through

a window

at just the

right angle

light dances

off of olive skin

in a million

colors

and I can see what

you're made of

Porch

It was a .500 weekend
About all I hope for these days
The Hogs pulled off the upset
and the Cowboys shit the bed

Somewhere in the world
you're buying a couch
and falling apart and
I'm going to let you

I'm busy, you know?
Busy sitting on this porch,
knee-deep in an existential crisis,
doing my best impression of a nihilist

My temple of hope
is ablaze

and you keep pissing
on the flames

Sunrise

The original abstraction

How did we come
to know the sky?

There was a first
to look up and wonder,

a first to question

There was a first
to offer an explanation

or rather, an interpretation

I imagine the first
conversation regarding the sky

I like to think they stopped short
of speaking with certainty

How could they?

There was a first
to decide for the rest of us,

a first to justify
deception

There was a first
to turn a blind eye

and then another

Jagged

I love you
in fifteen-second bursts
that feel like dreams
to those of us who
remember how

Do you know
this kind of longing?
The kind
That sets souls
to searching

the pages of books
and unfamiliar hands?
Those that do
almost always return
empty-handed

Just as I am now, here,
in the long shadow
of your love

Strange Weather

You sneak up

like strange weather

You tear the roof off

and send me spinning

You leave me contorted

and broken

Tangled in the trees

tangled in so

many, many

ways

Take these hands

and rebuild

all they

have destroyed

Make all things

whole again

Durable

The sunlight shining through
this pint of beer
reminds me that church
can be held anywhere

I have faith to spare
in what's proven durable,
and church didn't make
the cut

But this love of ours
has me speaking in tongues

Watching our children play,
soaking in their laughter,
I've no fear
of fiery judgment

I am born again

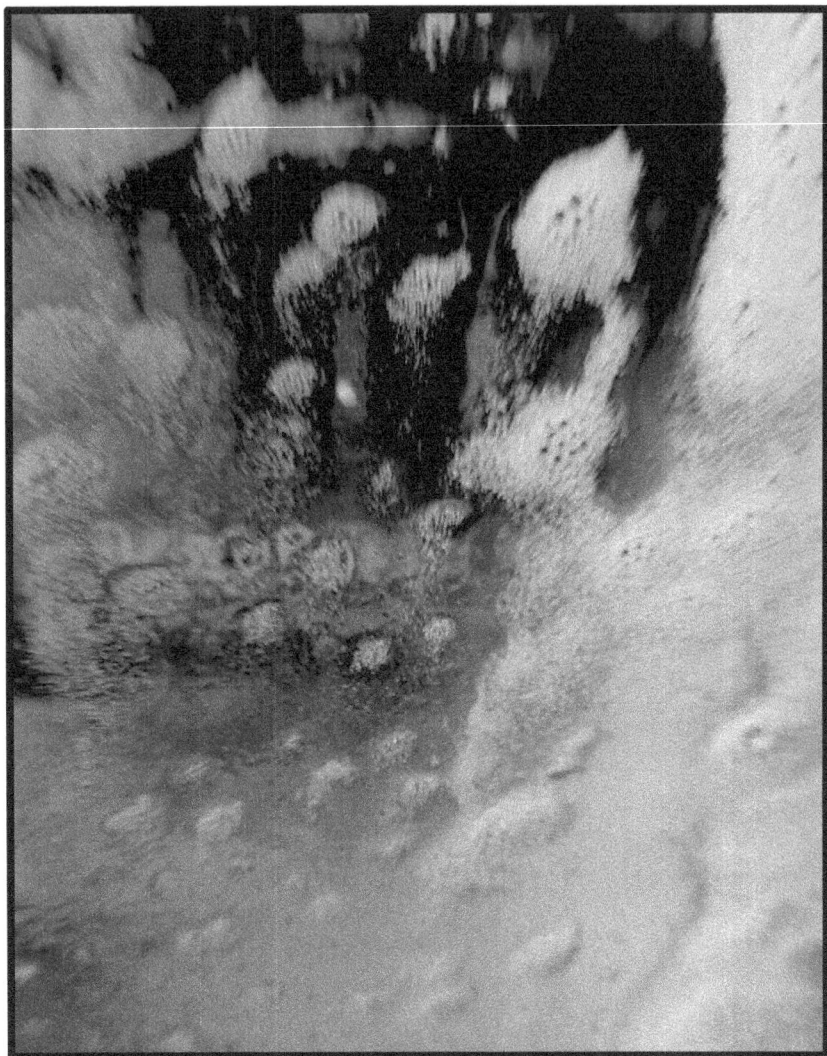

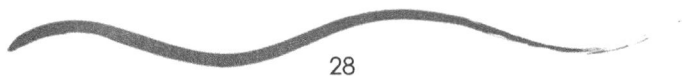

Ring

I've worn it every day since it was
placed on my finger so many years ago

before the hard times
When home was two bedrooms and cramped

and there was nothing to show
for our work and worry

Before cancer tore through
our lives

Before children
were a consideration

It wasn't expensive as far
as rings go

Not that that has anything
to do with worth

This morning, it was placed
into a hole in our door frame

and dropped like a quarter
in a jukebox

into the dark hollow of a wall
by a little girl

that regret was determined
to meet

She stared back at me,
eyes wet with tears,

knee deep in the kind of moment
I try so hard to save her from

She was forgiven almost immediately
and I cooled within the hour

I wear a new ring now

She laughs about it now

I do too

Float

The poems give me purpose,
like my children, my wife, and the dance I do
to provide

I push myself each day to pluck
something from the air to feed
the page,

just to watch it be lifted by the breeze,
carried up and away, into a world
that has no use for poetry,

and yet, is filled with poets that dream
of lucrative publishing contracts
and Atticus fame

Make no mistake, I crave recognition
I've tasted the victory of
a hero's validation,

and all that's left
to want is
more

Communion

A taste
You're lucky if you get one

Success is a flavor
infinitely complex

changing
over time

I keep forgetting
what it was I wanted

from all
of this

What was it again?
Communion?

At least that's what
I want to believe

Yes,

this and only this,

Communion

<u>Worth</u>

I'm thinking of jumping ship,
but I'm wondering what effect
it will have on my
mental wellbeing

What would life be without the depressives,
the hallmark card poets,
the passive-aggressive
vegans?

The ghost,
the romantic,
the songbird,
where did you go?

In all my searching,
I've found this to be true:

The work is always better
when you long for something

Recovery

I just got back
from the brink
to find
that nothing
much has changed
besides everything

The past is as real
as these two hands
carrying memories
all their own,
bringing close
and undoing

I'm 32 pounds lighter
because the virus
needed to take something
with it,
not unlike
everything else

I'm sucking air
like a fish
and keep
pushing away
thoughts of
heaven

Shift

The world passes by
through clear lines
in the etched glass
of my front door

The count is up to
three joggers and two walkers,
none with children or dogs,
all feeling better than I

A snoring Pit-lab at my feet
and a taste in my mouth
that I just can't seem
to brush away

The silence of this house
is unsettling but remains
because it isn't mine to break
Just as these bones, this skin;

none of it owned,
only borrowed
for a time

Still Here

I'm still here
to witness the world
and relay my observations
in poems you'll never read
They've crucified Woody Allen
I should've seen that one coming
I grind my teeth
thinking of February,
and now it hurts to chew

I'd sleep the rest of this week away
if life would let me
I'd disappear
into myself
and never come up for air
But that isn't how
any of this works

Poetry From Scratch

Arrive with nothing

Center your mind

Think about deep stuff

Pause for a selfie

Fix your hair

Does this expression

Convey

How broken

And creative I am?

Am I mysterious

And interesting enough

For your investment?

Worth your time?

The truth is

None of this

Has anything

To do with

Me

<u>Gone Fishing</u>

Time on the water

That's the secret

Don't let anyone
tell you otherwise

Of course, there's mystery

What pulls us
from the comfort of home
and into the world

Still, you must remain ready

You must remain wide-open
and vulnerable

You have to put some blood
in the water

You must be willing
to be consumed

completely

Sunken

Further down,
into the depths
of these sheets
into the darkness
of this room
No more eyes
No more sound

Only these eyes
this darkness
this slow breathing
In this disconnect
No God, no Devil,
just the cruel
mistake of consciousness

See now a sunken man
waiting for the weight
to lift,
for the vibrant colors
of life to come
seeping through the cracks
in the lies he tells himself

Nude

Lay bare and
offer up your throat

Is this not what it is
to be an artist?

To open oneself up
to public annihilation?

To dangle the heart
from a string

and offer up
the dagger?

I like
to think so

Especially when
reading a bad review

Grip

I feel like standing
beneath scalding water
until I'm stripped
to the bone

There's no shame
like trying to fit the mold
That's the stuff that
rots the soul,

the kind of thing
that that dims the light
in a person,
that kills a dream

So why is it so hard
to unclench the fist
when you already know
the hand is empty?

Unforgiven

I listened to your voice today
for the first time in a year
I needed to compare my memory
to the real thing

I was spot on
You still had your wits about you
You were concerned for me,
If I was caught in a storm

They hadn't
fucked us over yet
We weren't yet victims
of their egos and assumptions

All that fight undone
by one bad call
Would you
look at us now?

I,
the staggering drunk,
you,
returned to dust

The Challenge

To remember that poetry
is continuously present,
is the challenge

To recall in moments
of overwhelm that tax
the mind so heavily

that the poems remain,
waiting patiently
for you to realize

that all that's required
of you is a moment
of focus

where the heart,
hand, and mind
align

The Odds

Yes sir, I understand,
but the state STRONGLY
recommends this test
if there's any concern

The coffee's hot,
and this cloudless morning
has enough chill in the air
to keep me happy

My energy level
is nonexistent,
and this lends the world
a dream-like quality

The Bradford Pear
sways in the yard
beyond our fence
like a living van Gogh

The black and yellow
around the eyes
suggests your sinuses
have been inflamed a while now

I cough every third breath
Last night I woke
and my throat felt like
an open wound

When I spat in the sink
the pink saliva
that swirled down the drain
came as no surprise

The fever broke a while ago
I'm drenched in sweat
and searching for poetry
in this fucking mess

Your left ear is bulging
with infection
Are you sure you've
had no discomfort?

You're trying to talk
to me, and I'm trying
to be here
but I'm failing

My phone screen fills
with statistics
I tick the numbers up by one
to make room for myself

I silently add
life insurance totals
The chance of my demise is minimal,
but I have a way with defying the odds

We're just calling
to let you know
that the results
were negative

I watch our children
play with kinetic sand
and notice how the sunlight
seems to dance in their hair

and exhale

Layers

I'm stripping myself
from these words

layer by layer

Making more room
for you, for love

layer by layer

pulling away the ego,
the trivialities

layer by layer

Burning old furniture
Sinking the boats

layer by layer

Making more room
for you, for love

Shackled

Spend enough time in the company
of anything,

and eventually, you'll see
the chains;

that nothing moves freely
for long

As I jump between four
books of poetry,

four wildly different voices
rise from the pages

and lean too far one way
or the other;

Too earnest, too abstract,
too arrogant, too political

everyone's so worried
about being the voice of reason

that they forgot to write
anything interesting

Anxious Days

A cold ache in my chest,
that's where it lives

Sometimes manifesting
in my molars

jaws clinched
until stuck

This unease, this terrible sadness,
this wild craving for your hands

Everything inside is twisted up,
there's nowhere for the words to go

I keep a straight face,
I keep the war inside

Bath Time

Five decapitated mermaids
float by,

their heads settling
at the bottom of the tub

in the shape of a
crescent moon

As I pour water
through my daughter's hair,

I'm contemplating
the peace found in routines;

To bathe the child,
to rise in the morning,

to face the challenges
of work and living

Are these things
not holy?

What could be more
righteous

than selflessly giving time,
our numbered moments

without a single thought given to
the hope of reciprocity?

It is for you, my little birds,
for you, I answer the call

<u>Align</u>

When the grief lessened,
the pen, too, seemed to run dry

As if the mind
has no say in such things

As if it isn't enough
to want to create

While in alignment,
the poems drip from every surface

When out, things
are what they seem and nothing more

The words struggle to be free
as if forcing their way through thickets

bloody,
missing bits and pieces

Scattered Morning

These are the first words
I've written in twelve days

I'm boiling over with anxiety
but the pages remain blank

I've discovered how to overthink
my poems, like my songs, my life

It's Saturday and colder
than it should be in April

Outside, there's steady rain,
my children watch through the blinds

I'm thinking about
The Brian Jonestown Massacre

and the Camino de Santiago
They're unrelated

Just scattered thoughts
on a scattered morning,

grateful that the words
came easy

Take these eyes

and survey the horizon,

the endlessness

Hear the call

you've heard

all your life

Now answer

2060

This evening

I took an online quiz

that told me

the year I would die

based on lifestyle

and average life expectancy

It felt a lot

like cheating

on a test

White Wine Wisdom

I've never seen you from this angle
and I'm sorry, but it's changed
everything in how I feel

You've a life I know nothing about
and I exist in it the same as anything
providing temporary comfort

Last night before falling asleep,
I lost fifteen minutes staring at a picture of a high school
acquaintance turned junkie

We all make something of ourselves

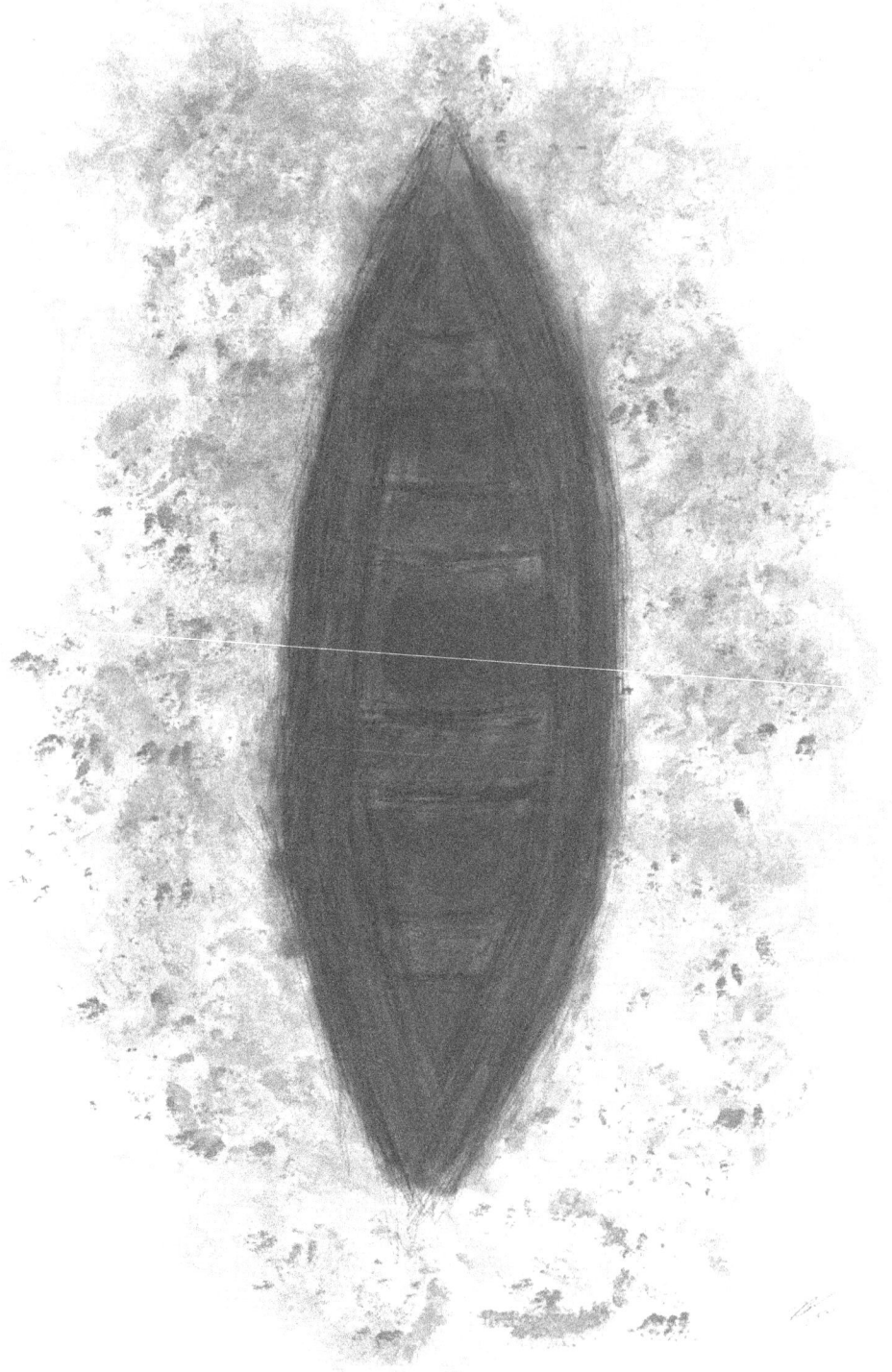

Uninspired Poem

I thought
it might be interesting
to write a poem
when I'm not feeling
much like
a poet:

I've been thinking,
I don't strive to feel happy
I strive to feel inspired
I'm inspired when I'm sad,
and, therefore, happiness
Is heartbreak

Thief

Perhaps it's the summer heat
that leaves me dried up,
void of ideas; even my thoughts
are melting together

I hate the humidity
and watching you
climb mountains
and raise a life from dust

or your toothless words
and their repetition
or the inconvenience
of your memory

or everything
you took when
you finally
went

Graphic Footage

The Blue light
of my phone floods the room,
the air filled with the whistle and snap
of exchanged gunfire

A child sleeping peacefully
less than a foot away
from the hand-held horrors of war
and a mind on fire

From this
eight-inch screen,
blissful ignorance
comes undone

Tell me,
where were you
when you found a tear
in the world you knew?

Who were you
after peeking through?

The Deal

That's it.
I'm going to write the bad ones

There will be nothing
erased

I struck a deal with myself
over a cup of coffee this morning,

and it's been decided that I will
inhabit this skin fully

Hustle & Bustle

On the back
and forth journey
of this concrete path

in the cold morning air
and beneath the glow
of the streetlight

in the chaotic sound
of roaring engines
and lives being lived

I thought of you

And my mind
filled-in your many mysteries,
and remembered

what it is
to fall in love
with an idea

Strange Magic

A glass balances
on my chest, hands
behind my head and I'm watching
as you tense;

as your hand grips with
impossible strength,
releases

This sacred ritual,
I feel I'm in a trance

what strange power
you hold over me

The Cost

It's day nine
and I'm wondering when
you're actually
on the other side

Clearheaded
and present
I don't nod off
at the keyboard

Yesterday evening
my children ran naked
into the rain, laughing
uncontrollably

and I was fully aligned,
mind and body,
in a moment as close
to perfect as I'll ever experience

I won't allow myself
to see these last three years
as wasted, but rather the unspoken cost
of loving you

The Hurt

If anyone asks,
It was cold turkey

I exorcised my pain,
spoke the words,

sent it
into the world

I haven't touched
the stuff since

The world is coming
into focus now

Color stops me
in my tracks

Steady rain
is overwhelming

Let me catch
my breath

I don't remember
how to do this,

how to get out
of the way

It all feels new
and terrifying

I'm trying to find
my footing

I stagger
to my feet

I draw air deep
into my lungs

And look back
at the aftermath

one last time
before I turn my face

into the
sun

What My Social Anxiety Used to Sound Like in My Head

Okay, I'm six in

which is way too many

and tomorrow

I will be again

for better or

for worse

and I'm watching

Midnight Mass

and I hope

to meet

Jacob for coffee

on Wednesday

and Travis for

Halloween Kills

but I wouldn't be surprised

if I found an out

because that's what I do

as I just want to make art

and I stay tired

and the moments

I truly crave companionship

are fleeting

and I'm not sure why

I ever make plans

So I'll probably

cancel tomorrow

maybe

Stained Cement

On most days
I occupy a seat
across from an
apartment complex
where a former soldier
suffering from PTSD
snapped and started
shooting up the parking lot

He only managed
to kill one person,
a sweet old lady
that I'd see around
from time to time,
she was shot walking out
of her apartment
to investigate the noise

After, the shooter was
killed by another tenant
The bodies were taken,
the blood stains scrubbed,
and life kept going
as it always does,
as if they were never here
an endless line of cars
passed by as if
nothing was out of the ordinary

Rushing Back

I'm doing 88 down I-40,
tears streaming,
time-traveling
on the back
of a song

I'm 34, and I've held
a man's hand as he died,
carried another to his grave,
and cradled the most beautiful children
just moments after their arrival

In other words, I've seen worlds
burned and born, and someone,
somewhere, has done the same,
only younger,
not that I was bragging

The years seemed
to have quickened
I've wept for the growing gap
between where I now stand and
the last time I heard
my father's voice

From suburban backyards
to forever,
we're an endless cycle of children
rushing back into the arms
of mothers and fathers
waiting just out of reach

Enough

Maybe this is all it'll take

for the wall between the words

and I to come crumbling down

I'm angry to feel myself giving up ground

to the anxiety I naively

believed to be under control

I've nothing to sell you,

nothing that would lure you in

I don't pander

All I have are these lines,

this nervous heart,

what I hope

is just enough

Purpose

Here is something
of the moment
I've pulled from
the air for you

From the bone dry
recesses of a mind
begging to burn again
with romantic ideas

that this world
could never live up to
To pull up
and out of my pessimism,

not with a mouthful
of self-help clichés,
but led again by my own
sparking curiosity

Here, little birds,
on the other side
of unimaginable loss
is what remains:

The lifting of the veil,
your once forgotten dreams

staring back

Happy Ending

Beneath a blanket of grey sky,
with an empty stomach
and a bursting heart
I watch your life pass by
like the highlight reel
of some game in which
I play no part
and have nothing on the line

I say this to say that I think of you
in quiet moments
and I know, without question,
that you are where you should be
and I am too
and that's all I've ever wanted
and the only happy ending
to hope for

<u>Devotion</u>

I'm in love
with the word
devotion

and I'm staring
at the beautiful
one

and there's
lightning inside
of me

and I've never
wanted anything
more

There's a song
in you that I'm
dying to hear

The World, The Wolf

I'm as sober as I've been
in three years

but the fluorescents in this office
are still hell on the eyes

A mid-20's slick-back
is wiping away tears

His supervisor was mean,
he feels attacked

I'm doing my best
to encourage

He's nice enough,
comes from money

Money that kept the world at
a safe distance until now

Now here he sits quaking in the
chair across from me

Knowing he's been had,
His face in his hands, sobbing

My eyes drift over
his shoulder

wondering how I tell this kid
that he's been living a lie

Outside my door,
the world paces back and forth

sensing fear,
licking its lips

How Much

How much I want these pages
to read differently

but here I am in this chair
in this office

in the arms of a panic that walks right
through Xanax

all because some entitled old man
made me feel like a shell

This isn't normal

*

I'm swimming against
the current

according to every quote I've read
about enlightenment

Isn't it fascinating how the heart
contorts to fit a life?

*

You know, I didn't write a poem
for almost a month

because nothing compared to the work
of Gregory Orr?

Is this nothing more than
an exercise in futility?

How long does it take to recognize
a trap?

What's Understood

All that matters now
are the steps forward

No matter how
plain the language

How flat the lines
sit on the page

How quickly they're
forgotten

Post-Meditation Poem #1

It isn't my eyes

There was nothing to see

beneath the mask

a glimpse of God

There was nothing to see

it isn't my eyes

a glimpse of God

beneath the mask

Center

There's a deep dissatisfaction
within me

It keeps me hungry, curious,
It pulls my introverted self

towards the world
in hopes of capturing

whatever may quell
such a feeling

Delivering me
to songs, to poems

wild, wide-eyed things
not meant for taming

but glimpses of the meeting
of the needle points

The elusive center
from which every moment

came bursting
into the world

Every joy,
every sorrow

Take this spirit

and set it to burning

I will no longer

settle for

survival

Sad Mother of the Retail World

There are so many

You really have no idea

Grandparents!

Great-Grandparents!

Struggling to care

for babies

Mothers

and Fathers

choosing that damn meth

over their children

I hope so much

that my boys

take the time

to mature

and become the fathers

they were meant to be

You seem like

a good man,

a good father,

there really should be

more men like you

I'm sorry, what do you mean

you can't refund this?

That's bullshit!

Are you fucking kidding me?

You've done nothing

to help me!

This place has forgotten

what customer service

looks like

and I'll be taking my business

elsewhere

Summer Night

The air outside is 82 degrees,
it blows through my fingers
and for a brief moment,
I'm 22 again, without burden

I realized tonight over
burgers and whiskey
that the reason I get so anxious
when leaving the house

is that I'm terrified
of the drive home
when my mind
is likely to wander

A perfect summer night
blowing through my hand
and feeling sure
that happiness is a brass ring

My foot presses down
on the accelerator,
trying to make it home to you
before I'm swallowed up

The Sinking

I'd convinced myself
that my mind is broken
and that the words had seemingly
gone where I
could not follow

I imagine
this could've been the result
of pouring
bottles of anything
down my throat every night

But now I'm dialed-in,
the signal coming through
loud and
clear

I've learned
that rebirth
looks and feels
a lot like sinking

but death can
be refused

The Lesson

Time heals nothing
of consequence,

but it dulls
the blade

That may sound
pessimistic

but the wound *is*
the lesson

and the burning
of the old life

and where the strength
is found

to begin again

Fur

A coyote was hit
on the 540 bridge
between Fort Smith
and Van Buren
in a way that made
disposal nearly impossible
The body settled
with its head
resting on the concrete ledge
like a pillow
I've passed it every day
for two months
Each day I caught
a glimpse of it coming apart
until there was nothing more than
than fur and bone,
and a steady flow of traffic
passing
on either side

Uvalde

I've given up on the world
I've been sold
useless systems,
useless prayers,
bullet riddled classrooms
Politicians on both sides
of the aisle,
baptized
in the blood
of our children

Search, search every inch
of the gore-soaked ground
Under whatever's left,
under every pair of little bloody shoes,
leave no stone, no body unturned
Surely,
surely there's still something
here to save

The Fall of Roe

I woke with a fire
in my lungs and
no desire to reach
for the phone dancing
across my nightstand

Roe v. Wade has been axed
My screen filled with
endless comments, confessions,
heartless celebrations,
genuine horror

My children are playing
A room away
Blissful ignorance
Unaware that an unelected few
have deemed them less

Our Country forces children
into the world
in the name of God
to see them mowed down
in classrooms by the dozens

I stand on the back patio
and draw air deep into my lungs,
eyes closed, face to the sun
Trying to push
the world away

Chain Breaker

I hydroplane every few feet
and there's no sign of the rain
letting up anytime soon
I wipe joy from my eyes,
Feeling some dry on my cheeks;
it lingers like the feeling of victory,
not long at all

I believe the possibility
of deliverance exists
on every gust of wind;
so don't look to me
for logic
When's the last time
you could breathe easily?

Was it before knowing
that every moment
comes with the possibility of
world-shattering finality?
Tell me,
what is it you wanted
after all this time

if not the freedom
to surrender
to all of life's possibilities?

Comes With

The smell of your hair
as you press your head
to my chest

the ease I feel
in this moment,
surely *this* is stronger

than death
Surely *this*
comes with

Realization

I've often wondered why
you entered my life

A threat?
A test?

Perhaps
both?

You'll now exist to me only
as a ghost, a memory,

something
tragic.

That's it,
isn't it?

You were meant to be
something tragic;

to haunt the mind,
the heart,

the poem

Dare

I miss cigarettes

but I'm not crazy
about the idea of
something killing me

So, I grind down
my days
while the TV
screams about
conmen, conspiracy,
coronavirus,
cock-pills

Earl Grey
I'm stacking
sober days
Covid death toll
hits half a billion

I close my eyes
and dream I'm standing
before a grove of trees
where something waits for me

to take one
more
step

Typical Evening

My father's ashes stare back
from the shelf

Family photos and ashes
Books of poetry and ashes
Cheap decor and ashes
Outdated Yamaha receiver and ashes
65-inch 4k screen and ashes
Sunday night and ashes

Surprisingly, it doesn't feel strange
I almost forget they're
there at times
My greatest pain,
momentarily
commonplace

In the Frozen Hours

I think of you in the frozen hours
when the head and eyes hurt most

How every step forward
is something lost

I can picture a world
where that infinite spiderweb

of choices placed me
in your path;

where, for some reason,
you felt compelled

to reconsider

19 16 22

Amnesiac Rising

Wake disoriented
to the chaotic room

the clothes
on the floor

and the sun through
the blinds

to whom do
these belong?

The edge of
the bed

now the edge
of the world

Rub the half-
remembered

dreams from
your eyes

familiar faces,
nameless ghosts,

Show me a heart
that isn't haunted

I don't remember
falling asleep

Never fully sure
I'm awake

Chernobyl x 10

I'm beginning to hear music
in my head again

like I did before the fracture

Across the world, a nuclear
plant is under siege

and the world watches
nervously

as the Russians continue shelling
the shit out of it

If this ends poorly, Europe
as we know it, ends

Would that make this
a swan song?

The Gift

I live not for risk
or adrenal rush

not for the company man
or his brass rings

I live for the song

For the perfect line

For the moment the muse rips
open the mystery

like a Christmas morning gift,
raising it to me, smiling, she says:

For you, the world

Outstretched

The dull ache
in my lower back
makes me wonder what
it would be like to be stabbed

There's a cure to this
tension readily available,
and a ghost
that calls to be free

If I turn
to the right too quickly,
I see a million stars
before I lose
my breath

The pain echoes
up my spine and radiates
out to the tips
of my outstretched
fingers

reaching up to a heaven
that never reaches
back

Hotel Art

Like a sneeze
upon the canvas

A hollowed out
confection

Reproduced by uninspired,
hourly paid brushes

Bargain bin
Monet

Discount
Dalí

For brand,
not heart

Financial
windfall

For the
artist,

A blessing?
A curse? Probably both

Does it
matter?

Put your
ear to it

listen
for a heartbeat

Then burn
time writing poetry

about nothing

Step Through

Remember

Remember why

Step-through
and be free from expectations,

from the unwinnable war

While you were chasing
the carrot on a string,

they were stealing
you blind

Be free of the hacks,
and secret soccer-mom nymphos

Be free of those feigning
enlightenment

What once was has
passed away

There's no returning

Step through

Watchers

We parked the car outside the cabin
and stepped into the chilly night,
heads swimming from too many
samples at the local winery

Something like sulfur
hung in the air,
the source hidden
among the trees

A guttural howl heard
the night before was enough
to send you scurrying
indoors – but tonight, we agreed to brave it

We put the kids to bed,
poured ourselves a drink
and sat beneath a blanket
on the back-porch swing

I took a deep breath of cold,
now clean-smelling air
and swirled my drink in its glass,
your head resting on my shoulder

A few moments later,
another howl heard somewhere
in the distance sent the nearby coyotes
into hysterics

I smiled,
pushing aside every rational
explanation that came to mind,
and opted

for wonder

Beyond

I thought I was finished with
these thoughts of endings

I've only
rearranged the room

How does one
move on?

How does one
not remain fascinated

with thoughts
beyond the flesh?

Tipping Point

Kill your dreams
if you want to see this through

The mind and bottle
manufacture false hope

and morning comes
bearing cruel reminders

of the price
paid in pursuit of oblivion

We dip our toes into
the void

and pray we keep
our footing

Cardinals

On a slow and winding road,
I spoke to you for the first time
in months
I thought of cardinals
and for a moment, pitied myself
for talking to the dead
I saw a documentary about
signs from the other side
and I want to ask for one
but always stop short
What would it mean to ask
and not receive in a moment like that?

When others tell you
they've felt a presence?
Would I hate them for it?
Would I hate you?
God?
I could never hate you

But maybe God,
in his infinite wisdom,
could cook up a better
explanation than his mysterious ways?
Then again, God never explains shit,
he leaves that to televangelists,

Cadillac-driving preachers,
youth ministers who
enjoy getting caught jerking-off
in public places
I like to think they kept Jesus
in their hearts the whole time

Death,
like all endings,
is a lie
When you exhaled your last,
somewhere,
you began again

Regarding the Passing of Time

There is no time to be still

There's only the running;

towards the grave,

into open arms,

burying my red-rimmed eyes

into your chest

into darkness

toward the sound

of your beating heart,

marking my minutes

by the sound

of your existence

2062

Update

I've rebuilt myself
entirely

and by doing so
added 2 years to my life

according
to this online test

Now

I've only to hope
that life

plays out
in such a way

that I'm glad
to still be here

Dora

Dora, you've changed so much
since we last spoke

I've always admired the confidence
to reinvent one's presentation

I've had the same haircut
for ten years

Dora, I'm terrible when it comes
to compliments,

I swear I'd never offer up
anything insincere,

but the way they have to fight their way
out of my mouth is exhausting

Dora, I once gifted a woman
hand-carved wooden figurines

that would hold each other forever
and a month later, found them

in a pile of trash behind
her driver's side seat

Dora, they say happiness
is a choice,

which tells me that some
are just better at turning away

I regret every slip of the tongue
and I remember them all

Dora, my childhood memories
feel like someone else's life

I miss everything
about simplicity

and the sound of my father having coffee
each morning while the rest of us slept

Dora, I've found infinite love
in the wide-eyed wonder of my children

My youngest carries a pumpkin
seed she believes to be holy,

because she knows something
I've long forgotten

Dora, I cracked open a bottle
and swallowed four years

Dora, I've come to rebuild

and I'm ready

to begin

Take this love

and build a boat

for the sinking

Take the offered hand

and come aboard

There's a light ahead

Acknowledgments

All my love to my beautiful wife, Kenzie, and my two wonderful daughters, Quinn and Scarlet. You three are the life and color of my world and enrich my life in ways I'll never be able to fully articulate.

Thank you to tara caribou, whose continued support and guidance means so much to me.

To my mother, Jacqueline, who continues to support and encourage me in all that I do.

To my father, Phillip, who keeps a watchful eye from above. We miss you every day.

And to Jacob Cotner, for your friendship, ear, honesty, and your willingness to jump into the deep end.

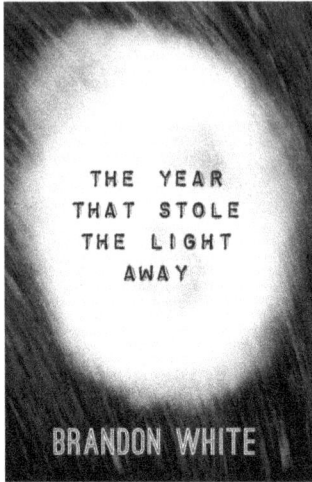

The Year that Stole the Light Away, the debut book of poems from Brandon White, is a remarkable journey through the depths of grief, heartbreak, and the first awkward footfalls back to a life rendered unrecognizable, yet budding with hope.

White guides us through a shared inevitability, offering a hand by which we might navigate the present darkness together and discover a way back to something that resembles home.

Real Big American Zen weaves the themes of an ache established in isolation, the depths of soul-searching, and unexpected humor from dark places. White ponders raising children in times of great uncertainty while digging into what it means to be an American during times of unprecedented political turmoil.

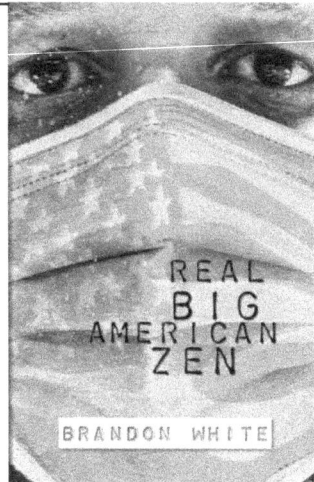

Slowly, making adjustments to a life in chaos and advancing over the uneasy path of a year swept up in pandemic.

Available online at Barnes and Noble, Amazon, and lulu. Signed copies available directly from the author at brandonwhitemusicandpoetry.com.

About the Author

Brandon White is a poet and songwriter from Fort Smith, Arkansas. His work has been featured in several anthologies and his debut collection of poetry, *The Year that Stole the Light Away*, released in 2020, has been highly acclaimed internationally. He released his follow-up collection, *Real Big American Zen,* in 2021.

White is also an accomplished songwriter, releasing several albums, EP's, and singles since 2007, with over 50 licensing deals for use of his work in retail environments and restaurants around the world.

He resides in Arkansas with his wife and twin daughters where he continues to write emotionally moving poetry and lyrics.

www.ingramcontent.com/pod-product-compliance
Lightning Source LLC
Chambersburg PA
CBHW031901090426
42741CB00005B/587